❖ GREAT LITTLE COOK B

Vegetarian COOKING

Barbara Rias-Bucher

Vegetarian cuisine is "in"!

Vegetarian food tastes delicious and offers plenty of variety. There are dishes which are simple and substantial, others which are exquisite and elegant, as well as hearty meals and light snacks, including sweet things to eat. Vegetarian food is becoming increasingly competitive with traditional cooking. The excellent products available can be combined in many imaginative ways and make cooking a pleasure.

Colour photographss by
Odette Teubner and Kerstin Mosny

AURA

CONTENTS

A little help to begin with

Going vegetarian does not just mean giving up meat and fish. It also means a healthy wholefood diet that offers plenty of variety. You will be using foods with which you are already familiar: vegetables, potatoes, rice, pasta, beans, peas, lentils, flour, dairy products and eggs. You can add to these at will with chick peas, tofu and perhaps even things you have grown yourself.

Here is some essential information about all these products to make it easier for you to begin, in case you are not yet familiar with some of these foodstuffs.

Nutrition-bomb: the potato

Potatoes play an important part in vegetarian cooking. They are particularly nutritious and provide the body with only as much energy – calories – as it needs. They contain very valuable plant protein. In combination with milk, cheese or eggs, for example, they provide more vital protein than a meal based around meat. Potatoes are rich in vitamins and minerals and high in fibre, which helps digestion and keeps the intestine healthy.

There are three types of potato. Which one you choose depends on whether you prefer waxy or floury potatoes for boiling with or without their skins, in stews, or for a golden topping. Particular varieties are most suitable for some dishes.

- Firm potatoes, such as Maris Peer, Pink Fir Apple and Belle de Fontenay, are ideal for salads, because they slice well.
- Firm-cooking potatoes, such as King Edwards, Maris Piper and Spunta, are suitable for frying or for chips because they do not break up easily and are fairly dry.

You can always find fresh fruit and vegetables in the market, often the exotic side by side with the home-grown. It is fun to compare what is on offer and take your time to pick out the best produce.

Every season offers many different vegetables, which make it easy to eat healthily and with plenty of variety.

● Floury potatoes, such as Vanessa, Pentland Squire and Cara, are used for mashing, dumplings, potato patties and creamy soups.

New potatoes are used as firm or firm-cooking varieties. Imported varieties arrive on the market early in the year and home-grown new potatoes are available from the end of May. The name and cooking-type is usually printed on the bags of pre-packed potatoes. If you buy unfamiliar potatoes loose, you can determine the cooking-type for yourself: cut a raw potato in half and rub the cut surfaces together. If water drips out, it is a firm-cooking potato. If the surfaces stick together, it is a starchy, floury variety of potato.

Eating potatoes in their skins is important for the fibre, most of which is found in the skin. Vitamins, however, are not lost when the potatoes are peeled, provided they are thinly peeled, because they are mostly located a few millimetres under the skin and inside the potato. You should always cut away green patches and sprouting parts, as they contain solanin, a natural poison that will not be destroyed by cooking.

Versatile vegetables

Vegetables do not always have to be cooked. In fact, about 40 per cent of the daily intake should be eaten raw – in salads or as in-between meal snacks. Raw vegetables make delicious starters, stimulating the digestive system and taking the edge off your hunger. They also contain plenty of fibre and have to be chewed well, so they are also good for the teeth. Vegetables that are suitable for eating raw include carrots, radishes, tomatoes, courgettes, peppers, fennel and celery, as well as many leaf vegetables, such as all kinds of lettuces, endive, radicchio, spinach, watercress and pak choi.

Beans should not be eaten raw (see page 6). Some wild mushrooms are also harmful if they are eaten raw. It is best to combine a vegetable that grows in the earth (bulb or root) with one that grows above ground (leaf vegetables, tomatoes, peppers). Use all the parts of the plant for your raw salad. For example, young radish leaves are also tasty, as are the finely chopped stalks of kohlrabi. Always prepare raw food just before eating it, otherwise you lose many valuable nutrients. Finally, do not forget to sprinkle something fresh over every cooked dish: raw grated vegetables, chopped fresh herbs or nuts.

Cereals

Cereals such as wheat, rye, barley, oats, millet, rice and maize provide the body with nearly everything it needs: high-value protein, satisfying carbohydrate, fibre, vitamins and minerals. They are also extremely versatile. They taste good in soups, braised, browned under the grill, as a side dish, as the basis for muesli and are essential for making dough. Your choice of cereal depends on how you want to cook it. You can make any kind of dough with wheat flour. Oats with their nutty taste are especially suitable for muesli. Millet and bulgur, also known as cracked wheat, are useful for quick side-dishes. You do not have to soak them and they cook in just 30 minutes. Rice is particularly easy to digest – exactly the right thing if you are just starting to eat food that is high in fibre and want your body to get accustomed to it gradually. Of course, you do not always have to use wholegrain cereals cooked from the raw materials. Many ready-made cereal products, such as wholemeal bread and pasta, pearl barley, semolina and white rice also have their place in the diet. You can compensate for the smaller quantity of fibre in pearl barley and white rice, for example, by increasing your intake of fruit and vegetables.

Pulses

Pulses have a very high protein content and also provide plenty of carbohydrate and fibre. Fresh beans and peas, as well as the edible-podded varieties, such as mangetout and sugar snap peas, are available for a short season and many varieties can also be bought frozen from most supermarkets. Dried beans are widely available throughout the year. Some varieties may be less familiar to you.

- Mung beans – ideal for fresh beansprouts – are small, dark green and have a visible white sprout. You should heat the sprouts for about 5 minutes to make them easily digestible. For example, you can stir-fry them in a little oil or steam them over boiling water. Note: raw beans are dangerous to health, so cook them thoroughly for at least 15 minutes.
- Chick peas are yellow to red in colour and irregular in shape. They are prepared like any other type of pulse.
- Flageolet beans are pale green, sometimes white, haricot beans and have the most delicate taste of all pulses.
- Red and brown lentils cook quickly and are particularly tasty. They are widely available from Indian supermarkets and health food shops.

Cereals play an important role in the diet and help to give it variety. There are many kinds you can eat, as for example, barley illustrated here.

Tofu with its high protein content is the ideal alternative to meat. It tastes good both in its natural state and also smoked or with herbs.

Tofu

Tofu, a soya bean product, is available in solid blocks or in a soft form, called silken tofu. It is rich in protein and valuable fatty acids, but does not contain sugar or cholesterol. The soya protein in tofu can even help to lower the cholesterol level in the blood.

Tofu provides very little carbohydrate and fibre, so it is best to combine it with vegetables, wholemeal products, brown rice, nuts or pulses. You can prepare it like meat – roast, grill, stir-fry or braise it. For making rissoles and similar dishes, it must be puréed or well mashed with a fork, so that the rissoles do not fall apart when they are fried.

Store tofu covered in water in a closed container in the refrigerator for up to a week. Change the water every day. Tofu can also be frozen. When it is thawed it becomes slightly porous, but the taste is barely affected. In fact, it has little flavour, but readily absorbs the flavours of other ingredients.

Sources of protein: dairy products

Plant foods in combination with milk, cheese, yogurt and other dairy products are particularly good for nutrition. The combination of dairy products and potatoes, pulses or cereals provides protein, which the body can use just as well as protein from meat or fish. It does not matter which dairy product you choose. They all have their advantages.

- Milk provides calcium and easily digestible protein.
- Yogurt and kefir, a yogurt-like product from the Middle East, are good for keeping the digestive system healthy.
- Sour milk products, such as crème fraîche, are also good for the digestion.
- Dairy products that are rich in fat, such as cream, crème fraîche and cheese, make vegetarian dishes substantial and satisfying.

Raw spring vegetables

Quick

Freshly prepared raw vegetables make a delicious starter. They take the edge off your hunger, stimulate the digestion and provide healthy fibre. You can vary the ingredients, but vegetables in season are best. In winter you can pep up the dish with green shoots that you have grown yourself.

Serves 4
350 g/12 oz mooli
300 g/11 oz carrots
1 bunch of radishes
2 eating apples, about 300g/11 oz
15 ml/1 tablespoon lemon juice
45 ml/3 tablespoons mild fruit vinegar
105 ml/7 tablespoons crème fraîche
60 ml/2 tablespoons sunflower oil
30 ml/2 tablespoons chopped fresh herbs
30 ml/2 tablespoons sunflower or pumpkin seeds
salt and freshly ground white pepper

Approximately per portion:
960 kJ/230 kcal
4 g protein, 16 g fat
18 g carbohydrate
7 g fibre

- Approximate preparation time: 30 minutes

1. Peel and grate the mooli and the carrots. Thinly slice the radishes. Cut the apples into quarters, core and grate them.

2. Mix all the ingredients with the lemon juice and arrange them attractively on four individual serving plates.

3. To make the dressing, thoroughly mix together the vinegar, crème fraîche and sunflower oil and season to taste with salt and pepper. Sprinkle the dressing over each plate of salad and garnish with the chopped fresh herbs and sunflower or pumpkin seeds. Serve the vegetables at room temperature.

Celery salad with oranges and nut sauce

Exquisite • Quick

Serves 4
3 oranges, about 500 g/1 1/4 lb
400 g/14 oz celery
juice of 1 small lemon
150 ml/1/4 pint low-fat yogurt
30 ml/2 tablespoons crème fraîche
15 ml/1 tablespoon finely ground walnuts or almonds
5 ml/1 teaspoon clear honey
5 ml/1 teaspoon sunflower oil
50 g/2 oz hazelnuts or walnuts
bunch of dill
freshly ground white pepper

Approximately per portion:
1,100 kJ/260 kcal
7 g protein, 15 g fat
23 g carbohydrate
5 g fibre

- Approximate preparation time: 20 minutes

1. Peel the oranges, separate the segments and cut them into pieces over a plate to catch the juice. Cut off the celery leaves and chop coarsely. Cut the celery sticks into 1 cm/1/2 inch pieces.

2. Mix together the oranges, the celery pieces and about half the celery leaves in a bowl.

3. To make the dressing, beat together the lemon juice, reserved orange juice, yogurt, crème fraîche, ground walnuts or almonds, honey and oil until smooth.

4. Pour the dressing over the salad and toss to coat well. Divide the salad between four individual serving plates.

5. Chop the nuts and finely chop the dill. Sprinkle the chopped nuts, dill and remaining celery leaves over the salad and season to taste with pepper.

Above: Celery salad with oranges and nut sauce
Below: Raw spring vegetables

Crudités

Rather time-consuming

Raw vegetables with a variety of dipping sauces make a delicious snack on a hot summer day.

Serves 4
65 g/2 1/2 oz mixed vegetables
4 spring onions
1 medium courgette, about 130 g/4 1/2 oz
4 large mushrooms
wholemeal rolls and butter, to serve

For the orange dip:
1 ripe avocado
1 orange
105 ml/7 tablespoons low-fat yogurt
15 ml/1 tablespoon chopped fresh parsley
salt and freshly ground white pepper

For the cheese dip:
115 g/4 oz full-fat cream cheese
50 ml/2 fl oz soured cream
15 ml/1 tablespoon milk
30 ml/2 tablespoons lemon juice
15 ml/1 tablespoon finely ground almonds
15 ml/1 tablespoon snipped fresh chives
salt
cayenne pepper

For the tofu dip:
115 g/4 oz tofu
50 ml/2 fl oz milk
15 ml/1 tablespoon double cream
1 clove garlic
bunch of fresh dill
1 gherkin
50 g/2 oz pistachio nuts or pumpkin seeds
5 ml/1 teaspoon capers
salt
cayenne pepper

Approximately per portion:
1,920 kJ/450 kcal
15 g protein, 33 g fat
21 g carbohydrate
6 g fibre

- Approximate preparation time: 50 minutes

1. For the orange dip, halve and stone the avocado and scoop out the flesh into a bowl. Thinly peel a 4 cm/1 1/2 inch long strip of orange rind and chop it. Squeeze the orange and mix the juice with the avocado flesh to prevent discolouration. Mash the avocado mixture with a fork. Mix in the yogurt, parsley and chopped orange peel and season to taste with salt and pepper.

2. For the cheese dip, mix together the cream cheese, soured cream and milk to a smooth paste. Add the lemon juice, ground almonds and chives. Season to taste with salt and cayenne pepper.

3. For the tofu dip, mash the drained tofu with the milk and cream or process in a food processor. Crush the garlic and finely chop the dill. Chop the gherkin and the pistachios or crush the pumpkin seeds. Stir the garlic, dill, gherkin, pistachios or pumpkin seeds and capers into the tofu mixture. Season to taste with salt and cayenne pepper.

4. Trim and chop the vegetables as required. Cut carrots, kohlrabi, radishes and cucumber into fingers. Divide cauliflower into florets. Cut peppers and fennel into strips. Slit thicker stalks lengthways if you wish. Cut the broccoli into florets and, if desired, peel the stalks and cut into fingers.

5. Trim the spring onions. Cut the courgette into fingers, halve or quarter the mushrooms, as desired.

6. Arrange all the prepared ingredients on a serving plate or divide them into portions. Put the dips into bowls. Serve with wholemeal rolls and butter.

Crudités and dips allow for many different colourful combinations, according to taste and the season.

Oat salad with spinach and tomatoes

Exquisite • Easy

This unusual salad has a deliciously fresh taste that makes it ideal for a light summer lunch or a substantial first course.

Serves 4
115 g/4 oz oats
250 ml/8 fl oz water
5 ml/1 teaspoon vegetable stock granules
2.5 ml/½ teaspoon dried thyme
250 g/9 oz spinach
300 g/11 oz tomatoes
1 spring onion
60 ml/4 tablespoons apple vinegar
15 ml/1 tablespoon cloudy apple juice
5 ml/1 teaspoon wholegrain mustard
30 ml/2 tablespoons wheatgerm oil
20 ml/4 teaspoons soured cream
2 tablespoons chopped fresh mixed herbs
salt and freshly ground black pepper

Approximately per portion:
690 kJ/160 kcal
6 g protein, 7 g fat
19 g carbohydrate
4 g fibre

- Soaking time: about 1 hour
- Approximate preparation time: 1 hour

1. Put the oats, water, stock granules and thyme in a saucepan and bring to the boil. Lower the heat, cover and simmer for 1 hour. Remove the saucepan from the heat and set aside for 1 hour.

2. Coarsely chop the spinach. Briefly blanch the tomatoes and peel, seed and dice the flesh. Thinly slice the spring onion.

3. To make the dressing, mix together the vinegar, mustard and oil and season to taste.

4. Mix together the oats, spinach, tomatoes, spring onion and dressing and divide between four serving plates. Put a teaspoon of soured cream on top of each plate and sprinkle with the herbs.

Bean salad with tomatoes and cheese

Easy

This substantial salad is a nourishing – and tasty – combination of pulses, vegetables and dairy products. Try to obtain sun-ripened tomatoes, which have the best flavour.

Serves 4
1 bunch of savory
300 g/11 oz green beans
300 g/11 oz frozen broad beans
250 ml/8 fl oz water
1 herbal teabag
45 ml/3 tablespoons mild fruit vinegar
15 ml/1 tablespoon double cream
15 ml/1 tablespoon herb mustard or Dijon mustard
45 ml/3 tablespoons corn oil
500 g/1¼ lb tomatoes
150 g/5 oz feta cheese
salt and freshly ground black pepper

Approximately per portion:
1,000 kJ/240 kcal
12 g protein, 13 g fat
18 g carbohydrate
4 g fibre

- Approximate preparation time: 35 minutes

1. Cut off the stalks from the savory and set the leaves aside.

2. Put the savory stalks, green beans, broad beans and water in a saucepan and bring to the boil. Lower the heat, cover and simmer for about 15 minutes, until the beans are tender.

3. Strain the beans, reserving the cooking water. Put the beans in a bowl and set aside to cool.

4. Bring the reserved cooking water to the boil again, add the teabag and remove the pan from the heat. Set aside for about 10 minutes to infuse, then remove and discard the teabag.

5. To make the dressing, mix the herbal tea with the vinegar, cream, mustard, and oil and season to taste with salt and pepper. Pour the dressing over the beans, toss to coat and divide the salad between four serving plates.

6. Dice the tomatoes. Chop the savory leaves. Crumble the cheese. Sprinkle the tomatoes, savory leaves and cheese over the salad.

Above: Bean salad with tomatoes and cheese
Below: Oat salad with spinach and tomatoes

Lentil salad

Rather time-consuming

Serves 4
250 g/9 oz green lentils
500 ml/17 fl oz water
5 ml/1 teaspoon vegetable stock granules
90 ml/6 tablespoon red wine vinegar or apple vinegar
90 ml/6 tablespoons corn oil
1/2 lemon
2 spring onions
1 green pepper, about 200 g/7 oz
1 carrot, about 150 g/5 oz
1 small bunch of fresh basil or parsley
salt and freshly ground black pepper

Approximately per portion:
1,400 kJ/330 kcal
16 g protein, 13 g fat
38 g carbohydrate
9 g fibre

- Approximate preparation time: 1 hour

1. Bring the lentils, water and stock granules to the boil in a saucepan. Cover and simmer for about 45 minutes, until they are tender.

2. Stir in the vinegar and oil. Season the lentils to taste with salt and pepper and set aside to cool.

3. Thinly peel the lemon and cut the rind into thin strips. Squeeze out the juice and mix it into the lentils, together with the rind. Divide the lentils between four individual serving plates.

4. Finely chop the spring onions. Core, seed and finely dice the green pepper. Grate the carrot. Tear the basil or parsley leaves off the stems. Reserve the leaves and chop the stems very finely.

5. Mix together the spring onions, green pepper, carrot and herb stems and sprinkle the mixture over the lentils. Transfer the mixture to a serving dish and garnish with the herb leaves.

6. Season the lentils again with salt and pepper and serve.

Cheese tartare with radishes and cucumber

Quick • Exquisite

Serves 6
300 g/11 oz Camembert cheese
25 g/1 oz butter, softened
15 ml/1 tablespoon double cream
1 onion
5 ml/1 teaspoon caraway seeds
5 ml/1 teaspoon mild paprika
bunch of radishes
6 tomatoes
1 cucumber
1 bunch of chives
15 ml/1 tablespoon chopped nuts
salt and freshly ground black pepper

Approximately per portion:
980 kJ/230 kcal
13 g protein, 18 g fat
6 g carbohydrate
3 g fibre

- Approximate preparation time: 30 minutes

1. Mash the Camembert cheese with a fork. Mix it with the butter and cream until smooth. Finely chop the onion and stir into the cheese mixture, together with the caraway seeds and paprika. Season to taste with salt and pepper.

2. Slice the radishes and cut the tomatoes into eight. Peel and coarsely grate the cucumber.

3. Arrange the radishes, tomatoes and cucumber separately on six individual serving plates and add the cheese mixture.

4. Snip the chives and sprinkle them over the vegetables. Sprinkle the cheese mixture with the chopped nuts and serve.

Above: Cheese tartare with radishes and cucumber
Below: Lentil salad

Raw carrots with grapes

Good value

Serves 3
500 g/1 1/4 lb carrots
250 g/9 oz white or black grapes
1 lemon
30 ml/2 tablespoons soured cream
5 ml/1 teaspoon clear honey
5 ml/1 teaspoon sunflower oil
50 g nuts, such as hazelnuts or almonds
small bunch of parsley
freshly ground black pepper
wholemeal toast and butter, to serve

Approximately per portion:
1,200 kJ/290 kcal
6 g protein, 13 g fat
35 g carbohydrate
8 g fibre

- Approximate preparation time: 20 minutes

1. Grate the carrots. Cut the grapes in half and remove the seeds if desired. Mix the carrots and grapes together. Squeeze the juice from the lemon.

2. To make the dressing, stir together the lemon juice, soured cream, honey and oil. Mix the dressing with the carrots and grapes. Divide the mixture between individual plates and season to taste with pepper.

3. Chop the nuts and finely chop the parsley. Sprinkle the nuts and parsley over the vegetables. Serve with hot wholemeal toast and butter.

Asparagus salad with alfalfa

Easy

Serves 4
25 g/1 oz alfalfa seeds
500 g/1 1/4 lb white asparagus
pinch of sugar
500 g/1 1/4 lb green asparagus
45 ml/3 tablespoons white wine vinegar or sherry vinegar
5 ml/1 teaspoon balsamic vinegar
5 ml/1 teaspoon English mustard
45 ml/3 tablespoons sunflower oil
5 cm/2 inch piece lemon rind
salt and freshly ground white pepper

Approximately per portion:
500 kJ/120 kcal
5 g protein, 12 g fat
4 g carbohydrate
4 g fibre

- Sprouting time for seeds: 3 days
- Approximate preparation time: 1 1/4 hours

1. Put the alfalfa seeds in a glass jar and cover them with warm water. Set aside for about 30 minutes. Cover the jar with gauze firmly attached with a rubber band and turn it upside down in the sink so that the water can drain. Then put the jar in a warm light place and leave the seeds to sprout for 3 days. Cover the seeds with warm water every day, leave to stand for a few minutes and again pour off the water. Alternatively, use a sprouter, following the manufacturer's instructions.

2. Peel the white asparagus. Cut off and discard the woody lower parts from both kinds of asparagus.

3. Fill a large saucepan three quarters full of water. Add the sugar and a pinch of salt. Bring the water to the boil. Add the white asparagus, bring back to the boil, lower the heat and simmer for 10 minutes. Add the green asparagus, bring back to the boil, cover and cook over a low heat for a further 8–10 minutes, until all the asparagus spears are tender.

4. Carefully remove the asparagus, drain and arrange side by side on a deep plate. Reserve the asparagus cooking liquid.

5. To make the dressing, mix together 75 ml/5 tablespoons of the reserved cooking liquid with the wine or sherry vinegar, balsamic vinegar, mustard and oil. Pour the dressing over the asparagus and set aside for about 30 minutes, until the asparagus has cooled completely.

6. Rinse the alfalfa sprouts in cold water and drain them. Finely chop the lemon peel. Sprinkle the alfalfa sprouts and lemon peel over the asparagus. Season the salad to taste with salt and pepper.

Above: Tasty Raw carrots with grapes stimulate the appetite.
Below: A pleasure not just for the eyes – Asparagus salad with alfalfa.

Vegetable broth with spelt dumplings

Rather time-consuming

Freshly made vegetable broth or stock is the basis for soups and sauces in vegetarian cooking. Spelt is an ancient wheat variety. It is available from some health food shops. Other cereals may be substituted (see Tip).

Serves 4–6
1 spring onion
15 ml/1 tablespoon corn oil
75 g/3 oz coarsely ground spelt
1.2 litres/2 pints water
75 g/3 oz wholemeal spelt flour
1 egg
15 ml/1 tablespoon soured cream
freshly grated nutmeg
250 g/9 oz leeks
350 g/11 oz carrots
1 Hamburg parsley root
1 bulb fennel, about 250 g/9 oz
250 g/9 oz celery
1 onion
1 clove garlic
bunch of parsley
a few sprigs of fresh thyme
5 ml/1 teaspoon white peppercorns
1 bay leaf
2 tomatoes
2 bunches of chives
salt and freshly ground white pepper

Approximately per portion:
950 kJ/230 kcal
10 g protein, 5 g fat
35 g carbohydrate
12 g fibre

- Approximate preparation time: 2 hours

1. Finely chop the spring onion. Heat the oil in a large saucepan. Add the spring onion and ground spelt and sauté, stirring constantly.

2. Pour in 150 ml/¼ pint of the water and bring to the boil, stirring until the mixture turns to a thick broth. Cover and cook, stirring occasionally, for about 20 minutes.

3. When cooked the mixture is so solid that it can hardly be stirred. Leave it to stand with the lid on for about 45 minutes, then mix it with the spelt flour, egg, soured cream and nutmeg and season to taste with salt and pepper.

4. Meanwhile, finely chop the leeks, carrots, Hamburg parsley, fennel, celery, onion and garlic. Tie the parsley and thyme into a bundle with the bay leaf.

5. Put the chopped vegetables, the herb bundle and the peppercorns into a saucepan. Add the remaining water and bring to the boil. Season with salt and simmer for about 30 minutes over a low heat.

6. Line a strainer with muslin. Strain the broth into a clean saucepan. To extract as much broth as possible press the vegetables and herbs with the back of a wooden spoon. Discard the contents of the strainer. Bring the broth to the boil again.

7. Use two teaspoons to shape about 16 dumplings from the dough. Cook one dumpling in the simmering broth until it rises to the top. If it keeps its shape, the dough is the right consistency. Otherwise, mix in more spelt flour 5 ml/1 teaspoon at a time. Cook the remaining dumplings in the same way.

8. Dice the tomatoes and snip the chives. Ladle the broth and the dumplings into individual soup bowls. Garnish with the tomatoes and chives and serve immediately.

Tip

You can prepare the vegetable broth in advance and freeze it in portions. It will keep tightly covered in the refrigerator for up to three days. Suitable vegetables are leeks, carrots, fennel, Hamburg parsley, celeriac and celery. You can flavour them as you like with herbs, garlic, bay leaves and/or juniper berries. You can vary the dumplings: you can make them with spelt or with wheat mixed with rye or oats. You can also use whole grains of millet or buckwheat. The dumplings freeze well. So you can prepare extra dumplings in advance.

Lentil soup with potatoes and herbs

Good value

Serves 4
1 small onion
5 ml/1 teaspoon wheatgerm oil
75 g/3 oz brown lentils
750 ml/1 1/4 pints vegetable stock
300 g/11 oz potatoes
150 ml/1/4 pint double cream
1 small bunch savory
1 small bunch chives
salt and freshly ground black pepper

Approximately per portion:
1,000 kJ/240 kcal
7 g protein, 13 g fat
24 g carbohydrate
5 g fibre

- Approximate preparation time: 1 hour

1. Finely chop the onion. Heat the wheatgerm oil, add the onion and lentils and sauté over a medium heat, stirring constantly, for a few seconds.

2. Pour in the vegetable stock, bring to the boil, cover and simmer over a low heat for 20–30 minutes, until the lentils are just beginning to soften.

3. Meanwhile, dice the potatoes. Add the potatoes to the lentils, bring the mixture back to the boil and cook the soup for a further 10–15 minutes, until the lentils and potatoes are tender.

4. Pour in the cream and re-heat, stirring constantly, to just below boiling point. Season the soup to taste with salt and pepper and serve immediately.

Vegetable soup with curry

Exquisite • Quick

This well-seasoned soup gently stimulates the appetite. Use just enough cayenne pepper to make it taste pleasantly hot, but without spoiling the flavour of the vegetables. If you do not want to buy the curry spices separately, you can use good quality ready-made curry powder to taste.

Serves 4
250 g/9 oz leeks
1 clove garlic
15 ml/1 tablespoon corn oil
2.5 ml/1/2 teaspoon ground turmeric
2.5ml/1/2 teaspoon ground cumin
2.5 ml/1/2 teaspoon ground coriander
2.5 ml/1/2 teaspoon ground ginger
2.5 ml/1/2 teaspoon saffron threads
pinch of cayenne pepper
750 ml/1 1/4 pints vegetable stock
2 tomatoes, about 400 g/14 oz
2 small courgettes, about 200 g/7 oz
1 bunch of parsley
salt

Approximately per portion:
280 kJ/67 kcal
4 g protein, 3 g fat
7 g carbohydrate
4 g fibre

- Approximate preparation time: 25 minutes

1. Thinly slice the leeks. Finely chop the garlic.

2. Heat the oil. Add the leek and garlic and fry over a medium heat, stirring constantly, for about 1 minute. Stir in the turmeric, cumin, coriander, ginger, saffron and cayenne pepper. Season to taste with salt and cook for a few seconds.

3. Pour in the vegetable stock, bring to the boil, cover and simmer over a low heat for 5 minutes.

4. Dice the tomatoes. Cut the courgettes into thin strips. Chop the parsley.

5. Add half the tomatoes and courgettes to the soup and cook until tender. Pour the soup into individual soup bowls and divide the remaining vegetables and the parsley between them. Serve immediately.

Above: A satisfying meal – Lentil soup with potatoes and herbs.
Below: Exotic – Vegetable soup with curry.

Green soup

Easy

Serves 4
500 g/1 1/4 lb mixed vegetables, such as carrots, celeriac, leeks and parsnips
1 small firm head of lettuce
250 g/9 oz spinach
1 large onion
30 ml/2 tablespoons sunflower oil
1 litre/1 3/4 pints vegetable stock
1.5 ml/1/4 teaspoon ground cumin
bunch of chives
25 g/1 oz sunflower seeds
200 ml/7 fl oz soured cream
cayenne pepper
salt and freshly ground white pepper

Approximately per portion
790 kJ/190 kcal
8 g protein, 13 g fat
10 g carbohydrate
7 g fibre

- Approximate preparation time: 40 minutes

1. Finely chop the mixed vegetables. Separate the lettuce leaves and cut them into thin strips. Chop the spinach. Finely chop the onion.

2. Heat the sunflower oil in a large saucepan. Add the vegetables and onion and sauté over a medium heat, stirring constantly.

3. Pour in the stock, bring to the boil and simmer for 2 minutes.

4. Add the lettuce and spinach and bring back to the boil. Season the soup to taste with salt and pepper and stir in the cumin.

5. Finely chop the chives and crush the sunflower seeds. Mix them with the soured cream and season well with cayenne pepper.

6. Ladle the soup into warm soup bowls. Add 15 ml/1 tablespoon of the spiced soured cream mixture to each bowl. Serve immediately and hand the remaining soured cream mixture separately.

Pearl barley soup with beetroot

Good value

Serves 4
1 small onion
1 clove garlic
75 g/3 oz pearl barley
5 ml/1 teaspoon corn oil
750 ml/1 1/4 pints vegetable stock
250 g/9 oz beetroot
120 ml/4 fl oz milk
105 ml/7 tablespoons double cream
1 egg yolk
pinch of freshly grated nutmeg
salt and freshly ground white pepper

Approximately per portion:
880 kJ/210 kcal
6 g protein, 12 g fat
21 g carbohydrate
4 g fibre

- Approximate preparation time: 1 hour

1. Finely chop the onion and garlic. Rinse the pearl barley in cold water and drain well.

2. Heat the oil. Add the onion, garlic and pearl barley and sauté over a medium heat for about 2 minutes. Add the vegetable stock. Bring to the boil, cover and simmer over a medium heat for about 20 minutes.

3. Trim the beetroot and reserve the young, fresh leaves. Peel and grate the root.

4. Add the beetroot to the soup and bring back to the boil. Cover and simmer over a low heat for about 5 minutes.

5. Beat together the milk, cream, egg yolk and about 30 ml/2 tablespoons of the hot soup. Stir this mixture into the soup and warm through, but do not allow it to boil or the egg yolk will curdle.

6. Stir in the nutmeg and season to taste with salt and pepper. Ladle it into warm soup bowls.

7. Finely chop the beetroot leaves, sprinkle them over the soup and serve immediately.

Above: Green soup is easy to make even for beginners.
Below: Colourful and full of flavour – Pearl barley soup with beetroot.

Spaetzle with vegetables

Rather time-consuming • Easy

Spaetzle – German pasta – can be quickly prepared from wholemeal noodles you have made yourself. They can be mixed with vegetables, sauces and cheese. Experienced spaetzle cooks spread the dough on a wooden board, shave off strips and put them into the cooking water with a wet knife. It is easier with a spaetzle-slicer, which you can buy in a specialist cookware shop. Vegetable spaetzle are very easy to prepare.

Serves 4
200 g/7 oz wholemeal flour
4–5 eggs
400 g/14 oz celeriac
1 kohlrabi, about 300 g/11 oz
250 g/9 oz carrots
1 small Savoy cabbage, about 500 g/1 1/4 lb
250 g/9 oz leeks
250 g/9 oz onions
25 g/1 oz butter
5 ml/1 teaspoon sunflower oil
120 ml/4 fl oz vegetable stock
bunch of parsley
salt and freshly ground white pepper

Approximately per portion:
1,900 kJ/450 kcal
25 g protein, 16 g fat
54 g carbohydrate
15 g fibre

- Approximate preparation time: 1 hour 10 minutes

1. To make the spaetzle, mix together the flour, a pinch of salt and 4 of the eggs. The dough should be viscous, so that marks made in it with a kitchen spoon fade slowly. If necessary, mix in more egg. Cover the dough and set aside.

2. Dice the celeriac, kohlrabi and carrots, reserving any tender leaves. Cut the cabbage and its stalk into strips. Trim the leeks and cut into fingers.

3. Thinly slice the onions and push out into rings. Heat the butter and oil in a frying pan. Add the onions and sauté over a low heat, stirring constantly, until they are soft and golden brown.

4. Bring a saucepan of well-salted water to the boil.

5. Bring the vegetable stock to the boil in another saucepan, add the vegetables and bring back to the boil. Cover and simmer over a low heat for 10–15 minutes, until they are tender, but still firm to bite.

6. Meanwhile cut off strips from the spaetzle dough spread out on a board or use a spaetzle-slicer and add them to the pan of boiling water. Cook the spaetzle until they rise to the top. Remove them from the saucepan with a slotted spoon and keep warm.

7. Mix together the vegetables, stock and spaetzle in a serving bowl and season to taste with salt and pepper.

8. Finely chop the parsley and the vegetable leaves. Sprinkle these and the fried onions over the vegetable spaetzle and serve.

Tip

You can vary the vegetables according to the season. You could also use green cabbage, red cabbage and fennel or asparagus, sugar snap peas and spring onions. In the summer and the autumn you could use tomatoes, courgettes and green beans.

Traditional German spaetzle served in a completely new way – with vegetables. If you are short of time, you can use ready-made spaetzle.

Braised oats with tomatoes

Rather time-consuming

Serves 4
200 g/7 oz oats
400 ml/14 fl oz water
5 ml/1 teaspoon vegetable stock granules
500 g/1 1/4 lb tomatoes
1 bunch of spring onions
1 small red pepper
50 g/2 oz mixed fresh herbs, such as parsley, thyme, marjoram or oregano
15 ml/1 tablespoon olive oil
pinch of sugar
105 ml/7 tablespoons soured cream
50 g/2 oz freshly grated Parmesan cheese
salt and freshly ground black pepper

Approximately per portion:
1,300 kJ/310 kcal
14 g protein, 12 g fat
37 g carbohydrate
6 g fibre

- Standing time: about 1 hour
- Approximate preparation time: 2 1/4 hours

1. Put the oats, water and stock granules in a saucepan and bring to the boil. Cover and cook over a low heat for 1 hour. Remove the pan from the heat and set aside for 1 hour.

2. Meanwhile, peel and dice the tomatoes. Cut the spring onions into short lengths. Seed the pepper and cut into thin strips. Coarsely chop the herbs.

3. Heat the oil. Add the spring onions and red pepper and sauté over a medium heat, stirring constantly, for about 3 minutes. Add the tomatoes, oats and the remaining cooking liquid and bring to the boil. Add the sugar and season to taste with salt and pepper. Cover and simmer over a low heat for about 5 minutes.

4. Stir in half the chopped mixed herbs. Transfer the mixture to warm individual serving plates and top each with soured cream. Sprinkle the remaining herbs and the Parmesan cheese on top and serve immediately.

Millet with green beans and feta cheese

Easy • Quick

Serves 4
600 g/1 lb 5 oz green beans
1 onion
1 clove garlic
1 bunch of savory
15 ml/1 tablespoon olive oil
200 g/7 oz millet
500 ml/17 fl oz vegetable stock
pinch of cayenne pepper
115 g/4 oz feta cheese
salt

Approximately per portion:
1,300 kJ/310 kcal
13 g protein, 10 g fat
40 g carbohydrate
10 g fibre

- Approximate preparation time: 50 minutes

1. Trim and slice the beans. Chop the onion and garlic. Finely chop the savory stalks and reserve the leaves.

2. Heat the oil. Add the onion, garlic and savory stalks and sauté over a medium heat. Add the millet and vegetable stock. Bring to the boil, cover and simmer over a low heat for about 15 minutes.

3. Add the beans and bring the mixture back to the boil. Cover and simmer for a further 15 minutes, until the beans are tender, but still firm to bite.

4. Season to taste with cayenne pepper and salt and transfer to individual serving plates. Crumble the feta cheese and sprinkle it, together with the savory leaves, over each plate. Serve immediately.

Above: Braised oats with tomatoes – an exquisite combination.
Below: A taste of Greece – Millet with green beans and feta cheese.

Quiche with tofu

Rather time-consuming • For guests

This hearty pastry with a savoury filling of vegetables, tofu and yogurt is ideal for many occasions. Served hot with a mixed salad, it is an excellent main dish. Warm or cold, it is perfect for a party buffet, brunch or as a snack with wine or beer. If you do not have time to make the pastry yourself, you can use frozen puff pastry. You can set it aside to thaw while you are preparing the filling.

Serves 5
150 g/5 oz wholemeal flour
22.5 ml/4 1/2 teaspoons iced water
75 g/3 oz butter, softened
300 g/11 oz tomatoes
1 bunch of spring onions
250 g/9 oz tofu
250 ml/8 fl oz yogurt
30 ml/2 tablespoons crème fraîche
50 g/2 oz freshly grated Emmental cheese
pinch of cayenne pepper
pinch of freshly grated nutmeg
50 g/2 oz crispbread, finely grated
25 g/1 oz sunflower seeds
salt

Approximately per portion:
1,800 kJ/430 kcal
16 g protein, 26 g fat
31 g carbohydrate
4 g fibre

- Approximate preparation time: 1 1/2 hours

1. To make the pastry, mix together the flour, salt, water and butter and knead lightly to a smooth dough. If necessary, add more water, drop by drop, until the dough is smooth.

2. Put the ball of dough into a 25 cm/10 inch quiche tin or springform tin and press it out until it covers the base. Then with your thumbs form a 4 cm/1 1/2 inch rim all round the sides. Chill in the refrigerator.

3. Peel the tomatoes and cut the flesh into slices. Trim and slice the spring onions. Drain and slice the tofu. Arrange the tofu, tomatoes and spring onions over the base of the pastry case.

4. Mix together the yogurt, crème fraîche, cheese, cayenne pepper and nutmeg, season to taste with salt and pour the mixture into the pastry case. Sprinkle over the grated crispbread and sunflower seeds. Bake in a preheated oven at 200°C/400°F/Gas 6 for 40 minutes.

Curd cheese and vegetable patties

Rather time-consuming

You can use vegetables in season, as desired, but they should not contain too much water. Juicy tomatoes or leaf vegetables, such as spinach, are less suitable. They must be very finely chopped, so that the dough does not fall apart and the cakes keep their shape during baking. If the dough is very wet, add more flour.

Serves 4
500 g/1 1/4 lb mixed vegetables, such as carrots, leeks, celeriac and courgettes
1 onion
1 bunch of parsley
250 g/9 oz low-fat curd cheese
2 eggs
115 g/4 oz wholemeal wheat flour
115 g/4 oz wholemeal crispbread, very finely crushed
pinch of cayenne pepper
pinch of freshly grated nutmeg
butter, for greasing
75 g/3 oz freshly grated Emmental cheese
30 ml/2 tablespoons olive oil
salt

Approximately per portion:
1,800 kJ/ 430kcal
26 g protein, 14 g fat
47 g carbohydrate
9 g fibre

- Approximate preparation time: 1 hour 35 minutes

1. Finely chop the mixed vegetables and the onion. Finely chop the parsley.

2. Mix together the vegetables, onion, parsley, curd cheese, eggs, flour and 25 g/1 oz of the crispbread and knead to make a smooth dough. Season well with cayenne pepper, nutmeg and salt.

3. Grease a baking sheet. Divide the dough into 12 pieces. With wet hands, shape each piece into a patty. Place the patties on the prepared baking sheet.

4. Sprinkle over the remaining the crispbread crumbs, the Emmental cheese and oil. Bake in a preheated oven at 180°C/350°F/Gas 4 for about 35 minutes. Serve with Raw spring vegetables (see page 8) or Raw carrots with grapes (see page 16).

Potato soufflé with nuts

Exquisite • Easy

Serves 4
800 g/1 3/4 lb floury potatoes
50 ml/2 fl oz vegetable stock
1 onion
1 bunch of fresh marjoram
120 ml/4 fl oz milk
3 eggs
115 g/4 oz freshly grated Gouda cheese
50 g/2 oz ground hazelnuts
15 ml/1 tablespoon wholemeal flour
2.5 ml/1/2 teaspoon cumin
50 g/2 oz butter
salt and freshly ground white pepper

Approximately per portion:
2,100 kJ/500 kcal
19 g protein, 31 g fat
38 g carbohydrate
7 g fibre

- Approximate preparation time: 1 3/4 hours

1. Dice the potatoes and put them in a saucepan with the vegetable stock. Bring to the boil, cover and simmer over a low heat for 20 minutes, until they are tender.

2. Chop the onion. Finely chop the marjoram.

3. Pour the milk over the cooked potatoes and beat vigorously with a whisk to a smooth purée. Set the potatoes aside to cool until they are lukewarm.

4. Separate the eggs. Mix the egg yolk, onion and marjoram into the potato mixture. Stiffly beat the egg whites and fold them in.

5. Mix together the cheese, hazelnuts, flour and cumin and season to taste with salt and pepper. Gently fold the mixture into the potato.

6. Use about one-third of the butter to grease a high-sided ovenproof dish. Spoon in the potato mixture and smooth the surface. Dot the remaining butter over the top.

7. Bake in a preheated oven at 180°C/350°F/Gas 4 for about 45 minutes.

Baked potatoes with creamy cheese filling

Easy

Filling, delicious and warming, baked potatoes are perfect for cold winter evenings.

Serves 4
8 potatoes about 1.5 kg/3 1/2 lb
5 ml/1 teaspoon caraway seeds
45 ml/3 tablespoons olive oil
200 g/7 oz blue-veined cheese, such as Gorgonzola or Roquefort
150 g/5 oz low-fat curd cheese
15 ml/1 tablespoon double cream
1 eating apple
2 spring onions
50 g/2 oz hazelnuts
rind and juice of 1/2 lemon
salt and freshly ground black pepper

Approximately per portion:
2,700 kJ/640 kcal
24 g protein, 31 g fat
66 g carbohydrate
11 g fibre

- Approximate preparation time: 1 hour 10 minutes

1. Cut the potatoes in half without removing their skins. Arrange them on a baking sheet, cut side upwards.

2. Mix the caraway seeds with salt and plenty of pepper and sprinkle the mixture over the potatoes. Sprinkle the potatoes with olive oil.

3. Bake the potatoes in a preheated oven at 180°C/350°F/Gas 4 for about 1 hour, until they are tender.

4. To make the filling, mash the blue-veined cheese with the curd cheese and double cream to a smooth paste.

5. Core and grate the apple and finely chop the spring onions. Chop the nuts and lemon rind.

6. Stir the apple, spring onions, nuts and lemon rind into the creamy cheese filling. Season with lemon juice, salt and pepper and serve with the potatoes.

The multi-purpose potato – Potato soufflé with nuts and Baked potatoes with creamy cheese filling.

Bulgur with aubergines

Rather time-consuming

This is the perfect combination of textures and flavours.

Serves 4
400 ml/14 fl oz water
200 g/7 oz bulgur
500 g/1 1/4 lb aubergines
250 g/9 oz tomatoes
1 onion
1 clove garlic
1 bunch of parsley
75 ml/5 tablespoons olive oil
105 ml/7 tablespoons crème fraîche
50 g/2 oz nuts
115 g/4 oz freshly grated Gouda cheese
cayenne pepper
1 bunch of basil
250 ml/8 fl oz yogurt
salt

Approximately per portion:
2,600 kJ/620 kcal
18 g protein, 38 g fat
13 g carbohydrate
5 g fibre

- Approximate preparation time: 1 1/2 hours

1. Bring the water to the boil in a large saucepan. Add the bulgur, bring back to the boil and cook over a medium heat for about 10 minutes, until all the liquid has been absorbed. Remove from the heat and set aside.

2. Dice the aubergines. Peel and dice the tomatoes. Chop the onion and chop or crush the garlic. Finely chop the parsley.

3. Heat the oil in a large frying pan. Add the aubergines, onion and garlic and sauté over a low, stirring frequently, heat for about 20 minutes.

4. Mix together the bulgur, aubergines, tomatoes, parsley, crème fraîche, nuts, cheese and a pinch of cayenne pepper and season to taste with salt.

5. Spoon the mixture into an ovenproof dish and bake in a preheated oven at 160°C/325°F/Gas 3 for about 45 minutes.

6. Finely chop the basil. Mix together the yogurt, basil, a pinch of salt and a pinch of cayenne pepper and serve with the bulgur.

Baked pasta

Easy

Serves 4
250 g/9 oz dried wholemeal pasta shapes, such as elbow macaroni
15 ml/1 tablespoon olive oil
2 large onions
1 kohlrabi, about 250 g/9 oz
115 g/4 oz mushrooms
300 g/11 oz tomatoes
120 ml/4 fl oz milk
120 ml/4 fl oz crème fraîche
150 g/5 oz freshly grated Gouda cheese
5 ml/1 teaspoon dried thyme
20 g/3/4 oz butter
1 bunch of chives
salt and freshly ground black pepper

Approximately per portion:
2,400 kJ/570 kcal
24 g protein, 31 g fat
50 g carbohydrate
9 g fibre

- Approximate preparation time: 50 minutes

1. Cook the pasta in lightly salted water according to the packet instructions until tender, but still firm to the bite. Drain and stir in the oil.

2. Finely chop the onions and kohlrabi. Chop the mushrooms. Peel and dice the tomatoes.

3. Mix together the pasta, onions, kohlrabi, mushrooms and tomatoes and spoon the mixture into an ovenproof dish.

4. Mix together the milk, crème fraîche, cheese and thyme, season to taste with salt and pepper and spoon this mixture on top of the pasta. Dice the butter and dot it over the mixture.

5. Bake in a preheated oven at 200°C/400°F/Gas 6 for about 30 minutes, until golden brown on top.

6. Snip the chives, sprinkle them over the pasta and serve.

Above: Satisfying when you are very hungry – Bulgur with aubergines.
Below: Baked pasta is easy to make even for beginners.

Vegetable soufflé

Rather time-consuming

Light and fluffy soufflés are not difficult to make – in spite of their reputation. However, they must be served immediately they have been taken out of the oven or they will collapse.

Serves 4
500 g/1 1/4 lb courgettes
250 g/9 oz spring onions
250 g/9 oz sauerkraut
2 cloves garlic
1 bunch of parsley
105 ml/7 tablespoons milk
65 g/2 1/2 oz wholemeal flour
5 ml/1 teaspoon paprika
pinch of freshly grated nutmeg
2 eggs
130 g/4 1/2 oz freshly grated Emmental or Gouda cheese
25 g/1 oz butter
salt and freshly ground white pepper

Approximately per portion:
1,400 kJ/330 kcal
20 g protein, 20 g fat
18 g carbohydrate
5 g fibre

- Approximate preparation time: 1 1/2 hours

1. Dice the courgettes and thinly slice the spring onions. Coarsely chop the sauerkraut. Chop the garlic and the parsley.

2. Thoroughly mix together the milk, flour, paprika and nutmeg and season to taste with salt and pepper. Separate the eggs. Stir the egg yolks into the flour mixture. Mix in the courgettes, spring onions, sauerkraut, garlic and fresh parsley.

3. Beat the egg whites until they form stiff peaks and carefully fold them into the mixture. Sprinkle in the cheese and gently mix well.

4. Spoon the mixture into an ovenproof dish with fairly high sides and smooth the top. Dot the surface with the butter. Bake in a preheated oven at 180°C/350°F/Gas 4 for 45 minutes, until golden on top. Serve immediately.

Lentil soufflé with nuts

Exquisite • Rather time-consuming

This unusual and melt-in-the-mouth soufflé is both highly nutritious and full of flavour.

Serves 4
1 onion
15 ml/1 tablespoon corn oil
50 g/2 oz red lentils
25 g/1 oz wholemeal flour
500 ml/17 fl oz water
5 ml/1 teaspoon vegetable stock granules
5 ml/1 teaspoon dried savory
1 bunch of parsley
1 bunch of chives
4 eggs
50 ml/2 fl oz soured cream or crème fraîche
50 g/2 oz ground nuts
75 g/3 oz freshly grated Emmental cheese
butter, for greasing
salt and freshly ground white pepper

Approximately per portion:
2,100 kJ/500 kcal
30 g protein, 24 g fat
39 g carbohydrate
9 g fibre

- Approximate preparation time: 1 3/4 hours

1. Chop the onion. Heat the oil in a saucepan, add the onion and sauté until it is translucent. Stir in the lentils and flour. Gradually stir in the water. Add the stock granules and savory and season to taste with salt and pepper. Bring to the boil, cover and cook over a low heat for 15 minutes. Remove the pan from the heat and set aside until the lentils are lukewarm.

2. Finely chop the parsley and chives. Separate the eggs. Mix the herbs, egg yolks and soured cream or crème fraîche into the lentils.

3. Beat the egg whites until stiff peaks form and carefully fold them into the lentils. Mix together the nuts and grated cheese and sprinkle them on the lentils. Gently mix together. Grease an ovenproof dish with fairly high sides and spoon in the lentil mixture, smoothing the top.

4. Bake in a preheated oven at 180°C/350°F/Gas 4 for about 45 minutes, until golden on top. Serve immediately.

Soufflés require a bit of time, but they are well worth it.
Above: Vegetable soufflé
Below: Lentil soufflé with nuts

Baked courgettes with wheat

Rather time-consuming

A light summer meal, which is easy to prepare and quick to cook. It is not difficult even for inexperienced cooks to succeed with this dish and it will be enjoyed by all who like grains prepared in an unusual way and are accustomed to plenty of fibre. If you have only just started eating whole foods, use the more easily digested brown rice instead of wheat. In summer you can also prepare this dish with ripe beefsteak tomatoes and fresh herbs, such as rosemary or sage.

Serves 4
200 g/7 oz wholegrain wheat
375 ml/13 fl oz water
600 g/1 lb 5 oz small courgettes
1 lemon
60 ml/4 tablespoons olive oil
1 onion
2 cloves garlic
5 leaves fresh sage
300 g/11 oz red or green peppers
105 ml/7 tablespoons crème fraîche
pinch of cayenne pepper
65 g/2 1/2 oz freshly grated Parmesan cheese
2 carrots, about 200 g/7 oz
salt and freshly ground black pepper

Approximately per portion:
1,800 kJ/430 kcal
15 g protein, 23 g fat
43 g carbohydrate • 10 g fibre

- Soaking time: about 1 hour
- Approximate preparation time: 1 1/2 hours

1. Put the wheat grains and water in a saucepan, cover and set aside to soak for 1 hour. Add a pinch of salt and bring to the boil. Cover and simmer over a low heat for 1 hour.

2. Cut the courgettes in half lengthways. Place the halves on a baking sheet, cut side upwards.

3. Cut off a wafer-thin slice of lemon rind about 2.5 cm/1 inch long and set aside. Squeeze the juice from the lemon.

4. Mix together 60 ml/4 tablespoons lemon juice and 45 ml/3 tablespoons of the olive oil and pour it over the courgettes. Season to taste with salt and pepper.

5. Bake the courgettes in a preheated oven at 180°C/350°F/Gas 4 for about 30 minutes, until they are just tender.

6. Meanwhile, chop the onion and garlic. Finely chop the sage leaves, together with the lemon rind. Seed the peppers and dice the flesh.

7. Heat the remaining oil. Add the onion and garlic and sauté over a low heat, stirring constantly, until translucent. Add the sage and lemon rind, the peppers, wheat grains and any remaining cooking liquid and the crème fraîche. Bring to the boil, cover and cook over a low heat for 5 minutes.

8. Stir in the remaining lemon juice, the cayenne pepper and grated cheese and season to taste with salt.

9. Arrange the courgettes and wheat on warm plates. Grate the carrots and sprinkle them on top and serve immediately.

A tasty dish that is always enjoyed – Baked courgettes with wheat.

Red cabbage rolls with millet

Rather time-consuming

You can make filled vegetarian rolls with virtually any leaf vegetables. However, it is easiest to work with vegetables that have large firm leaves, such as red cabbage – as in the recipe – white cabbage, Savoy and Chinese cabbage.

Serves 6
115 g/4 oz millet
150 ml/¼ pint water
5 ml/1 teaspoon vegetable stock granules
400 g/14 oz tomatoes
115 g/4 oz mushrooms
2 onions, about 200 g/7 oz
1 clove garlic
15 ml/1 tablespoon dried oregano
115 g/4 oz freshly grated Emmental cheese
1 red cabbage, about 1 kg/2¼ lb
45 ml/3 tablespoons corn oil
105 ml/7 tablespoons crème fraîche
1 bunch of parsley
salt and freshly ground black pepper
potatoes boiled in their skins, to serve

Approximately per portion:
1,200 kJ/290 kcal
11 g protein, 17 g fat
20 g carbohydrate
9 g fibre

- Approximate preparation time: 1½ hours

1. To make the filling, put the millet, water and stock granules in a saucepan and bring to the boil. Cover and simmer over a low heat for about 25 minutes.

2. Peel the tomatoes and dice the flesh. Finely chop the mushrooms. Chop the onions and garlic.

3. Mix the tomatoes, mushrooms, onions, garlic, oregano and cheese with the millet. Season to taste with salt and pepper.

4. Bring a pan of well-salted water to the boil, add the cabbage and boil for 5–6 minutes, until 12 leaves can be easily separated from it.

5. Remove the cabbage and let it cool slightly. Reserve the cooking liquid. Cut the cabbage leaves away from the stalk with a sharp knife. Carefully separate 12 leaves and trim the thick veins flat. Cut the remaining cabbage into eight and set aside.

Tip

The cabbage leaves are easier to separate and roll up if you cook the firm cabbage in fast boiling water. If you are using vegetables with looser leaves, such as Chinese cabbage, simply cut off the leaves and blanch them until they are just soft.

6. Spread the 6 largest leaves side by side on a work surface and place the 6 smaller leaves on top of them. Divide the filling between the leaves. Fold the leaves over, then roll them up and tie with kitchen string.

7. Heat the oil in a large saucepan. Add the cabbage rolls and fry on all sides over a low heat. Pour in 120 ml/4 fl oz of the reserved cooking liquid. Bring to the boil, cover and simmer over a low heat for about 10 minutes.

8. Add the remaining cabbage and crème fraîche to the pan and bring back to the boil. Cover and cook over a low heat for a further 10 minutes. Chop the parsley and sprinkle it over the cabbage rolls. Transfer to a warm serving dish and serve immediately with potatoes boiled in their skins.

White cabbage with chive rice

Easy • Good value

Serves 2
300 ml/$^1/_2$ pint water
150 g/5 oz long grain rice
1 small white cabbage, about 500 g/1$^1/_4$ lb
300 g/11 oz tomatoes
1 large onion
30 ml/2 tablespoons corn oil
$^1/_2$ bunch of basil or parsley
1 bunch of chives
30 ml/2 tablespoons crème fraîche
salt

Approximately per portion:
2,100 kJ/500 kcal
12 g protein, 19 g fat
74 g carbohydrate
14 g fibre

- Approximate preparation time: 45 minutes

1. Bring the water to the boil in a large saucepan. Add the rice and a pinch of salt, cover and cook over a very low heat for about 40 minutes, until the rice is tender, but still firm to the bite and all the water has been absorbed. Fluff it up with a fork and set aside.

2. Meanwhile, cut the cabbage into eight. Peel the tomatoes and dice the flesh. Chop the onion.

3. Heat the oil in a large saucepan, add the onion and sauté, stirring constantly, until translucent. Add the cabbage and the tomatoes. Bring to the boil, cover and simmer over a low heat for about 5 minutes, until the cabbage is tender, but still firm to bite. Season to taste with salt.

4. Finely chop the basil and chives. Mix the chives into the rice.

5. Spoon the vegetables and rice on to individual warm plates, top the vegetables with a little crème fraîche and sprinkle with basil. Serve immediately.

Winter vegetables with mushroom bulgur wheat

Good value

Serves 3
500 g/1$^1/_4$ lb mixed vegetables, such as leeks, celeriac, carrots and Hamburg parsley
1 bulb fennel, about 250 g/9 oz
2 large onions
200 g/7 oz mushrooms
30 ml/2 tablespoons lemon juice
60 ml/4 tablespoons sunflower oil
250 g/9 oz bulgur wheat
500 ml/17 fl oz vegetable stock
5 ml/1 teaspoon caraway seeds
105 ml/7 tablespoons single cream
bunch of parsley
salt and freshly ground white pepper

Approximately per portion:
2,500 kJ/600 kcal
17 g protein, 24 g fat
80 g carbohydrate
11 g fibre

- Approximate preparation time: 45 minutes

1. Dice the mixed vegetables. Cut off the fennel leaves and set them aside. Cut the fennel bulb in half, then cut into strips across the fibres. Chop the onions.

2. Chop the mushrooms and mix them with the lemon juice.

3. Heat 15 ml/1 tablespoon of the oil. Add the bulgur wheat and fry, stirring constantly. Add the stock, bring to the boil, cover and cook over a low heat for 20 minutes.

4. Heat the remaining oil, add the onions and sauté until translucent. Add the mixed vegetables and fennel and sauté, stirring constantly, for a few seconds. Season to taste with salt and pepper and stir in the caraway seeds. Add the cream, cover and cook over a low heat for about 5 minutes.

5. Mix the mushrooms into the bulgur wheat and heat through. Finely chop the fennel leaves, sprinkle them over the vegetables and bulgur wheat and serve.

Above: A satisfying dish for the cold season – Winter vegetables with mushroom bulgur wheat.
Below: White cabbage with chive rice – simple to prepare.

Asparagus with potatoes and dill cream

Easy

You can prepare this delicately flavoured and mouth-watering dish with plump white asparagus, as shown here, or with the thinner green variety.

Serves 2
800 g/1¾ lb small new potatoes
1 kg/2¼ lb asparagus
5 ml/1 teaspoon butter
1 bunch of dill
1 spring onion
115 g/4 oz low-fat yogurt
30 ml/2 tablespoons crème fraîche
30 ml/2 tablespoons cream cheese
salt and freshly ground white pepper

Approximately per portion:
1,800 kJ/430 kcal
23 g protein, 10 g fat
73 g carbohydrate
18 g fibre

- Approximate preparation time: 45 minutes

1. Cook the potatoes in their skins in a small quantity of water for about 15–20 minutes, until they are tender.

2. Peel the asparagus stalks, if necessary, and cut off the woody parts. Bring a pan of well-salted water to the boil with the butter. Add the asparagus, bring back to the boil and simmer over a medium heat for 10–20 minutes, until tender, but still firm to bite.

3. Finely chop the dill, reserving a few sprigs for the garnish. Thinly slice the spring onion.

4. Mix together the yogurt, crème fraîche and cream cheese. Mix in the chopped dill and spring onion. Season with salt and pepper.

5. Drain the asparagus. Arrange it on warm plates with the potatoes. Garnish with the reserved dill sprigs and serve immediately with the dill cream.

Carthusian dumplings with tomato salad

Good value

The fresh taste of the tomato and feta cheese salad perfectly complements the crispness of the fried Carthusian dumplings. This would make a delicious summer lunch or supper – preferably eaten *al fresco*.

Serves 4
4 day-old wholemeal rolls
about 250 ml/8 fl oz milk
pinch of cayenne pepper
pinch of freshly grated nutmeg
2 small eggs
45 ml/3 tablespoons crushed crispbread
5 ml/1 teaspoon dried oregano
60 ml/4 tablespoons olive oil
1 kg/2¼ lb tomatoes
1 bunch of chives
1 bunch of basil
45 ml/3 tablespoons balsamic or red wine vinegar
75 g feta cheese
salt and freshly ground black pepper

Approximately per portion:
1,600 kJ/380 kcal
15 g protein, 18 g fat
40 g carbohydrate
8 g fibre

- Approximate preparation time: 30 minutes

1. Grate off the crusts from the rolls. Cut the rolls in half lengthways and arrange them side by side in a flat dish. Heat the milk with the cayenne pepper, nutmeg and a pinch of salt to just below boiling point and pour it over the rolls. Set aside to soak for about 2 minutes, until they have absorbed the liquid, but are not so soft that they fall apart.

2. Beat the eggs. Mix the crispbread with the oregano on a plate. Heat 30 ml/2 tablespoons of the oil in a frying pan.

3. Dip the rolls first into the beaten eggs and then into the crispbread crumbs and fry in the hot oil over a medium heat for 5 minutes on each side.

4. Slice the tomatoes. Chop the chives and basil. Arrange the tomato slices on a plate and sprinkle the herbs, vinegar and the remaining oil over them. Crumble the feta cheese over the tomatoes. Season the tomatoes with salt and pepper and serve with the Carthusian dumplings.

Above: Prelude to spring – Asparagus with potatoes and dill cream.
Below: A hearty favourite – Carthusian dumplings with tomato salad.

Millet dumplings with tomato sauce

Rather time-consuming

It is only the dumplings in this recipe that take rather a lot of work to prepare. If any dumplings are left over, they freeze well and after thawing can be served in tomato sauce or vegetable broth with freshly chopped herbs.

Serves 5
200 g/7 oz millet
450 ml/15 fl oz water
5 ml/1 teaspoon vegetable stock granules
500 g/1 1/4 lb sauerkraut
3 onions
1 bunch of parsley
2 eating apples, about 300 g/11 oz
30 ml/2 tablespoons lemon juice
500 g/1 1/4 lb tomatoes
2 sage leaves
45 ml/3 tablespoons corn oil
1 bay leaf
120 ml/4 fl oz cloudy apple juice
2 eggs
40 g/1 1/2 oz wholemeal flour
30 ml/2 tablespoons crème fraîche
1/2 bunch of chives
salt and freshly ground black pepper

Approximately per portion:
1,600 kJ/380 kcal
12 g protein, 12 g fat
49 g carbohydrate
8 g fibre

- Approximate preparation time: 1 1/4 hours

1. Put the millet, water and stock granules in a saucepan and bring to the boil. Cover and simmer over a low heat for 30 minutes. Remove the pan from the heat and set aside until the millet is lukewarm.

2. Meanwhile, drain the sauerkraut. Chop the onions. Finely chop the parsley. Core and dice the apples and mix them with the lemon juice to prevent discolouration. Peel the tomatoes and dice the flesh. Finely chop the sage leaves.

3. Heat 15 ml/1 tablespoon of the oil. Add about one third of the onions and sauté over a medium heat until translucent. Add the sauerkraut, bay leaf and apple juice and season to taste with salt and pepper. Bring to the boil, cover and cook over a low heat for 20 minutes. Stir in the apples and cook for a further 10 minutes.

4. To make the dumplings, bring a pan of well-salted water to the boil. Mix together the millet, eggs, half the remaining onions, the parsley, flour and a pinch of salt. With damp hands shape 10 dumplings from the dough. Add to the boiling water and cook, uncovered, over a very low heat for 15 minutes. The water should be barely simmering.

5. To make the tomato sauce, heat the remaining oil in a large saucepan. Add the remaining onions and sauté until translucent. Add the tomatoes and sage and cook over a high heat, stirring constantly, for about 5 minutes. Stir in the crème fraîche and season to taste with salt and pepper.

6. Snip the chives. Remove the dumplings from the pan with a slotted spoon, drain well and place them on individual warm plates. Arrange the sauerkraut beside them. Pour the sauce over the dumplings, sprinkle with the chive rings and serve immediately.

Variation
Instead of millet, you can use buckwheat. You can cook the sauerkraut with vegetable stock instead of apple juice. Instead of apples, you can add about 300 g/11 oz coarsely grated carrots to the sauerkraut.

Millet dumplings with tomato sauce are tasty and satisfying, as well as being easy to make.

Potato mould with broccoli

For guests • Rather time-consuming

This mould is particularly suitable for a dinner party. It cooks for so long in steam that you can comfortably prepare the other dishes. In addition, it does not spoil the texture if it remains in its mould after it has cooked. The basis of a mould is flour, bread, other ingredients which absorb liquid well or – as in this recipe – mashed potatoes

Serves 6
800 g/1 3/4 lb broccoli
400 g/14 oz floury potatoes
1 onion
1 bunch of marjoram or parsley
3 eggs
105 ml/7 tablespoons creme fraîche
30 ml/2 tablespoons milk
pinch of freshly grated nutmeg
25 g/1 oz wholemeal flour
115 g/4 oz freshly grated Emmental cheese
50 g/2 oz ground walnuts
salt and freshly ground white pepper

For preparing the mould:
butter
50 g/2 oz crispbread, crumbled

Approximately per portion:
1,500 kJ/360 kcal
17 g protein, 21 g fat
24 g carbohydrate
8 g fibre

- Approximate preparation time: 2 1/2 hours

1. Chop the broccoli. Finely dice the potatoes. Put the broccoli and potatoes in a pan and add a little salted water. Bring to the boil, cover and cook over a low heat for about 15 minutes, until tender. Strain the vegetables and mash with a fork.

2. Finely chop the onion and marjoram. Stir them into the mashed vegetables. Separate the eggs. Mix together the egg yolks, crème fraîche, milk and nutmeg, season to taste with salt and pepper and stir into the mashed vegetable mixture.

3. Beat the egg whites until stiff peaks form and fold them into the vegetable mixture. Fold in the flour, cheese and nuts. Grease a mould with butter and coat the base and sides with crumbled crispbread. Spoon the vegetable mixture into the mould and cover with a lid or a double thickness of securely tied foil.

4. Put the mould in a large saucepan and add sufficient boiling water to reach two thirds of the way up the side of the mould. Cover and steam over a low heat for about 1 hour 10 minutes. When the mould is cooked, leave it to stand in its mould for a further 10 minutes. Loosen around the top edge with a knife and turn out on to a serving plate.

Cheese and nut waffles with leek salad

Rather time-consuming • Exquisite

These waffles are ideal for entertaining guests. You can prepare the batter and leeks beforehand. Then the waffles are fried together at the table and everyone is served directly from the waffle pan.

Serves 4
For the leek salad:
750 g/1 lb 10 oz thin leeks
30 ml/2 tablespoons corn oil
pinch of sugar
250 ml/8 fl oz vegetable stock
15 ml/1 tablespoon fruit vinegar
salt
cress, to garnish

For the waffles:
200 g/7 oz wheat grains
250 ml/8 fl oz milk
105 ml/7 tablespoons soured cream
2 eggs
115 g/4 oz freshly grated Gouda cheese
115 g/4 oz ground hazelnuts
10 ml/2 teaspoons dried thyme
pinch of freshly ground nutmeg
oil, for greasing

Approximately per portion:
2,500 kJ/600 kcal
26 g protein, 36 g fat
43 g carbohydrate
13 g fibre

- Approximate preparation time: $4\frac{3}{4}$ hours of which 3 hours are standing time

1. To make the salad trim the leeks and cut them into fingers.

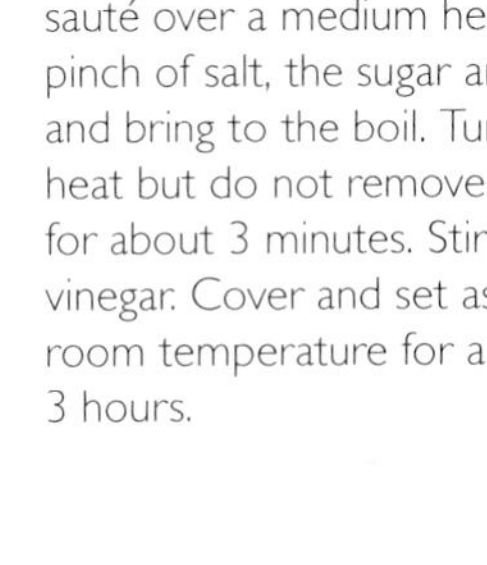

2. Heat the oil. Add the leeks and sauté over a medium heat. Add a pinch of salt, the sugar and stock and bring to the boil. Turn off the heat but do not remove the pan for about 3 minutes. Stir in the vinegar. Cover and set aside at room temperature for a further 3 hours.

3. To make the waffles, coarsely grind the wheat and mix together with the milk, soured cream, eggs, grated cheese, nuts, thyme and nutmeg and season to taste with salt and pepper.

4. Shortly before eating, sprinkle the cress over the leek salad. Oil the cooking surface of the waffle pan. Put 22.5 ml/$4\frac{1}{2}$ teaspoons of the batter in the pan at a time and fry each waffle for 3–4 minutes.

Tomato pasta with Savoy cabbage

Easy • Rather time-consuming

Home-made pasta takes some time. It is important that the wholemeal flour is sifted. This recipe is based on wholemeal pasta made with eggs; if you do not eat eggs, use about 105 ml/ 7 tablespoons cold water instead. With wholemeal flour it is difficult to be exact about amount of egg yolk or water needed. Therefore, you should knead the dough by hand, so that you can tell when it has reached the right consistency.

Serves 4
225 g/8 oz wholemeal flour
2 eggs
75 ml/5 tablespoons olive oil
2–4 egg yolks
1 Savoy cabbage
1 large onion
1 clove garlic
400 g/14 oz tomatoes
105 ml/7 tablespoons crème fraîche
1 bunch of chives
2 sprigs of fresh thyme
salt and freshly ground black pepper

Approximately per portion:
2,400 kJ/570 kcal
25 g protein, 30 g fat
51 g carbohydrate
12 g fibre

- Approximate preparation time: about $2^3/_4$ hours

1. To make the pasta, mix together the flour, eggs, 15 ml/1 tablespoon of the olive oil and a pinch of salt. Gradually knead in as much egg yolk as is required to make the dough smooth and elastic. If necessary, beat the egg yolk towards the end. The dough should not crumble. It should be elastic and give when touched. It should not stick to the fingers.

2. Shape the dough into a ball and wrap it in greaseproof paper. Set aside at room temperature for about 30 minutes.

3. Divide the ball of dough into four. Using your hands, knead each piece on a floured work surface or feed it through a pasta machine by hand. Then roll out the pieces into very thin sheets. Place them on clean tea towels and leave to dry for about 10 minutes. Cut each sheet of dough into ribbons. Place them on clean tea towels and leave them to dry for about 1 hour.

4. Meanwhile, trim the Savoy cabbage, cut it into eight, then cut into thin strips. If desired, also cut up the stalk and the thick-veined leaves and use these too. Chop the onion and garlic. Peel the tomatoes and dice the flesh.

5. Heat 45 ml/3 tablespoons of the oil in a large frying pan. Add the onion and garlic and sauté until translucent. Add the cabbage and sauté, stirring constantly, over a medium heat. Cover the frying pan and cook the cabbage over a low heat until the pasta is dry.

6. Heat the remaining oil in a saucepan. Add the tomatoes and the crème fraîche, cover and cook over a low heat.

7. Cook the pasta in a large saucepan of well-salted boiling water for 1–2 minutes, until it is tender, but still firm to bite.

8. Season the cabbage and tomatoes to taste with salt and pepper. Finely chop the chives. Pull the thyme leaves of the stems.

9. Place the cabbage on individual warm plates and sprinkle with the chives. Drain the pasta ribbons and mix them with the tomatoes, tossing them thoroughly. Arrange them next to the cabbage and sprinkle with thyme leaves. Serve immediately.

Tomato pasta with Savoy cabbage is a dish that takes some time to prepare, but it is not difficult and the combination of colours is very appetizing.

Pasta with beansprouts

Easy

Serves 2
40 g/1 1/2 oz mung beans
1 onion
15 ml/1 tablespoon olive oil
105 ml/7 tablespoons crème fraîche
30 ml/2 tablespoons lemon juice
25 g/1 oz freshly grated Parmesan cheese
250 g/9 oz dried wholemeal pasta, such as tagliatelle
2 tomatoes
1 bunch of chives
salt and freshly ground black pepper

Approximately per portion:
3,500 kJ/830 kcal
33 g protein, 35 g fat
89 g carbohydrate
15 g fibre

- Sprouting time for mung beans: 4 days
- Approximate preparation time: 40 minutes

1. Put the mung beans in a glass jar, cover them with warm water and set aside for about 30 minutes. Cover the jar with gauze or muslin firmly fastened with an elastic band and turn it upside down in the sink, so that the water runs out. Put the jar in a warm light place and leave the seeds to sprout for 4 days. Every day cover the beans with warm water, leave to stand for a few minutes and pour it away.

2. Chop the onion. Heat the oil, add the onion and sauté over a medium heat until translucent. Add the beansprouts and crème fraîche. Bring to the boil, cover and cook over a low heat for about 5 minutes.

3. Stir in the lemon juice and the Parmesan cheese, season to taste with salt and pepper, cover and keep warm.

4. Cook the pasta in a large pan of well-salted water for 8–10 minutes, until tender, but still firm to bite. Drain and mix the pasta with the beansprouts, tossing well.

5. Dice the tomatoes. Snip the chives with kitchen scissors.

6. Place the pasta on individual warm plates and top with the tomatoes and chives. Serve immediately.

Pasta with vegetables and breadcrumbs

Good value • Easy

Serves 4
600 g/1 lb 5 oz mixed vegetables, such as carrots, courgettes, turnip and swede
1 onion
50 g/2 oz wholemeal bread
60 ml/4 tablespoons olive oil
pinch of cayenne pepper
400 g/14 oz dried wholemeal small pasta, such as fusilli
30 ml/2 tablespoons double cream
50 g/2 oz freshly grated Parmesan cheese
30 ml/2 tablespoons chopped fresh mixed herbs
salt

Approximately per portion:
2,300 kJ/550 kcal
23 g protein, 17 g fat
78 g carbohydrate
12 g fibre

- Approximate preparation time: 40 minutes

1. Finely chop the vegetables. Chop the onion. Crumble the bread finely.

2. Heat 30 ml/2 tablespoons of the oil in a frying pan. Add the breadcrumbs and fry over a low heat, turning constantly, until they are crisp.

3. Heat the remaining oil in a saucepan. Add the onion and sauté over a low heat until translucent. Add the vegetables and sauté over a low heat, stirring and tossing frequently, until tender. Season with cayenne pepper, cover and keep warm.

4. Cook the pasta in a large pan of well-salted water until it is tender, but still firm to bite. Stir 60 ml/4 tablespoons of the cooking water, the cream and cheese into the vegetables.

5. Drain the pasta and mix it with the vegetables and the toasted breadcrumbs. Arrange the pasta on individual warm plates, sprinkle the herbs over it and serve immediately.

Above: Pasta with beansprouts
Below: Pasta with vegetables and breadcrumbs

Potatoes with a thick vegetable sauce

Quick • Easy

This sauce is an ideal way to use up offcuts and trimmings of green vegetables that you probably would have thrown away. It tastes good made with any vegetable leaves – radish leaves, turnip tops, or carrot tops. You can also use the remains of herbs, onions or leeks, celery and fennel leaves. All these ingredients, with the exception of carrot tops and turnip tops, become tender as quickly as spinach. Carrot and turnip tops require about 7 minutes. This dish can also be made with spinach alone.

Serves 2
500 g/1 1/4 lb small potatoes
500 g/1 1/4 lb spinach
400 g/14 oz tomatoes
2 spring onions
30 ml/2 tablespoons sunflower oil
20 ml/4 teaspoons creme fraîche
1/2 bunch of parsley
salt and freshly ground white pepper

Approximately per portion:
3,000 kJ/710 kcal
16 g protein, 49 g fat
49 g carbohydrate
15 g fibre

- Approximate preparation time: 25 minutes

1. Put the potatoes, without peeling them, in a saucepan. Add a little boiling salted water and cook for 10–15 minutes, until tender.

2. Meanwhile, coarsely chop the spinach. If desired, use the harder stalks as well. Peel the tomatoes and dice the flesh. Cut the spring onions into smaller pieces.

3. Heat the sunflower oil in a large frying pan. Add all the chopped vegetables and sauté over a high heat, stirring constantly, for about 2 minutes. Season to taste with salt and pepper.

4. Add the crème fraîche, bring to the boil and cover. Turn off the heat, but do not remove the pan for about 2 minutes.

5. Finely chop the parsley. Drain the potatoes, put them on to individual warm plates and cut them in half. Spread the sauce over them and sprinkle with parsley. Serve immediately.

Variation
Instead of spinach, you can use carrot tops, leftover kohlrabi, celeriac and/or courgettes. Grate these vegetables as finely as possible and prepare the sauce as described above.

Tip

It is not necessary to blanch tomatoes before you skin them. If the tomatoes are really ripe you can simply pull off the skins. If that does not work, use the following method: Run the blade of a small sharp knife over the whole surface of the tomato. Use strong pressure and slant the blade slightly, so that the skin is not torn. Leave the tomatoes to stand for at least 3 minutes or until you have prepared the other ingredients. Then pull off the skin with the knife. Always remove the stalks and green tomato pips, because both contain small amounts of harmful solanin.

Potatoes with a thick vegetable sauce – there is no better way to use up leftover vegetables.

Lentil rice with spinach-tofu curry

Exquisite • Rather time-consuming

This is a spicy dish for those who like exotic food. The curry tastes best if you mix the different spices yourself. Of course, you can also use ready-made curry powder, but beware of the quality. Cheap curry powder may often have an unpleasant taste.

Serves 4
1 small onion
5 ml/1 teaspoon butter
115 g/4 oz long grain rice
115 g/4 oz brown lentils
500 ml/17 fl oz vegetable stock
1 kg/2¼ lb fresh spinach
2 cloves garlic
250 g/9 oz tofu
50 g/2 oz walnuts
15 ml/1 tablespoon ground turmeric
5 ml/1 teaspoon ground cumin
5 ml/1 teaspoon ground coriander
2.5 ml/½ teaspoon ground ginger
pinch of cayenne pepper
75 ml/5 tablespoons sunflower oil
juice of 1 lemon
105 ml/7 tablespoons low-fat yogurt
15 ml/1 tablespoon crème fraîche
1 bunch of parsley
salt

Approximately per portion:
2,000 kJ/480 kcal
22 g protein, 25 g fat
40 g carbohydrate
11 g fibre

- Approximate preparation time: 1 hour 10 minutes

1. Chop the onion. Melt the butter in a saucepan. Add the onion and sauté until translucent. Add the rice, lentils and stock. Bring to the boil, cover and simmer over a low heat for 45 minutes, until the rice and the lentils are just tender.

2. Trim the spinach. Chop the garlic. Drain the tofu and dice it. Coarsely chop the walnuts. Mix the turmeric, cumin, coriander, ginger, cayenne pepper and a pinch of salt in a small bowl.

3. Heat 45 ml/3 tablespoons of the oil in a frying pan. Add the spice mixture, garlic and tofu and stir-fry over a medium heat until the tofu is golden all over. Remove from the heat and keep warm.

4. Heat the remaining oil in the frying pan. Add the spinach and nuts, in batches, and stir-fry over a medium heat, until the spinach is wilted and bright green. Mix each batch of the spinach with the tofu and keep warm.

5. Stir in the lemon juice and season to taste with salt and cayenne pepper if necessary. Transfer to individual warm plates with the cooked lentil rice.

6. Beat together the yogurt and crème fraîche. Finely chop the parsley. Top the curry with a spoon of the yogurt mixture and sprinkle with the parsley. Serve immediately.

Variation
Instead of spinach you can use the same quantity of turnip tops, pak choi or Chinese cabbage.

Tip

When buying spinach, look for firm, green, unblemished leaves. It is best used as fresh as possible and should never be stored for longer than one day. It must be washed in several changes of water to remove all traces of soil and grit. Shake the leaves dry. Cut out the central ribs if they are tough, but this is not usually necessary with young spinach.

Lentil rice with spinach-tofu curry tastes best with home-made curry powder.

Yeast dumpling with apricot sauce

Rather time-consuming

A traditional main dish in a number of European countries, this is known as clootie dumpling in Scotland. It is easy to make using whole foods – wholemeal flour, minimal sweetening and fresh fruit according to the season.

Serves 4
300 g/11 oz wholemeal flour
1/2 packet dry yeast
25 g/1 oz raw sugar
250 ml/8 fl oz lukewarm milk
2 eggs (at room temperature)
grated rind of 1/2 lemon
500 g/1 1/4 lb apricots, stoned
105 ml/7 tablespoons unsweetened fruit juice
5 ml/1 teaspoon ground cinnamon
salt
softened butter, for greasing
flour, for dusting

Approximately per portion:
1,700 kJ/400 kcal
16 g protein, 7 g fat
71 g carbohydrate
4 g fibre

- Approximate preparation time: 1 3/4 hours of which 1 hour is standing time

1. Mix the flour with the yeast and 5 ml/1 teaspoon raw sugar. Add the milk, eggs, grated lemon rind and a pinch of salt. Mix thoroughly for 5 minutes. Cover the dough and set aside at room temperature for about 45 minutes, until it has doubled in size.

2. Wring out a tea towel in hot water and spread butter over it. Then sprinkle it with flour. Put the dough on it, formed into a large dumpling and set aside for a further 15 minutes.

3. Bring a large pan of salted water to the boil. Wrap the tea towel loosely around the dumpling and tie it at the top to form a loop. Stick a kitchen spoon handle through this loop and hang the dumpling over the saucepan, so that the whole dumpling is in the water. Cover and simmer for about 45 minutes over a medium heat.

4. To make the sauce, purée the apricots with the fruit juice and lemon juice. Mix the cinnamon with the remaining sugar. Cut the dumpling into portions, sprinkle with cinnamon, pour on the sauce and serve immediately.

Rice soufflé with damsons

Easy • Exquisite

This is an uncomplicated dessert that is easy to make. If you serve a good soup beforehand, this rice soufflé makes a satisfying meal, particularly enjoyed by children. You can choose whatever fruit is available and fully ripe.

Serves 4
200 g/7 oz round grain rice
500 ml/15 fl oz milk
grated rind of 1/2 lemon
750 g/1 lb 10 oz damsons
50 g/2 oz butter
50 g/2 oz raw sugar
4 eggs
butter, for greasing
finely crushed crispbread
salt

Approximately per portion:
2,400 kJ/570 kcal
16 g protein, 22 g fat
78 g carbohydrate
5 g fibre

- Approximate preparation time: 1 hour 40 minutes

1. Put the rice, milk, lemon rind and a pinch of salt in a saucepan and bring to the boil. Cover and simmer for 45 minutes over a low heat, until the rice is tender. Set aside to cool until it is lukewarm.

2. Meanwhile, halve, stone and chop the damsons.

3. Beat the butter with the sugar until it becomes pale and fluffy. Separate the eggs. Stir the egg yolks, then the rice – a spoon at a time – into the butter mixture. Beat the egg whites until very stiff and fold them into the mixture.

4. Grease a high-sided ovenproof dish with butter and sprinkle crushed crispbread on the base and sides. Spoon the soufflé mixture into the dish and bake in a preheated oven at 180°C/350°F/Gas 4 for about 45 minutes.

Fruit salad with yogurt sauce

For guests

For the full flavour of this sweet salad the fruit must really be fully ripe. This ensures that it contains plenty of natural sugar so that you need to add only very little extra sweetening.

Serves 4
600 g/1 lb 5 oz mixed fruit in season, such as loganberries, blackberries, raspberries or strawberries, cherries and peaches or damsons, pears and grapes or apples, bananas and pineapple
1 small lemon or orange
1 avocado
30 ml/2 tablespoons clear honey
150 ml/$^1/_4$ pint low-fat yogurt
30 ml/2 tablespoons double cream
75 g/3 oz nuts, such as almonds or hazelnuts

Approximately per portion:
1,700 kJ/400 kcal
7 g protein, 27 g fat
34 g carbohydrate
6 g fibre

- Approximate preparation time: 40 minutes

1. Core, stone and otherwise prepare the fruit as appropriate and cut larger fruit into bite-size pieces.

2. Cut off and a reserve a strip of lemon or orange rind and squeeze the juice. Mix the juice with the prepared fruit.

3. Cut the avocado in half, remove the stone and scoop out the flesh. With a fork, mash the avocado flesh with the lemon or orange rind, honey, yogurt and cream. Alternatively process the avocado flesh, lemon or orange rind, honey, yogurt and cream in a food processor. Chop the nuts.

4. Arrange the fruit on individual plates and pour on the sauce. Sprinkle the nuts on top.

Peach sorbet

Exquisite

White peaches are particularly aromatic and flavoursome and are the best to use for this elegant sorbet, but of course you can substitute yellow peaches or nectarines.

Serves 6
250 g/9 oz peaches
30 ml/2 tablespoons clear honey
250 ml/8 fl oz unsweetened fruit juice
30 ml/2 tablespoons lemon juice
2 fruit teabags
250 ml/8 fl oz boiling water
150 g/5 oz strawberries, raspberries or blackberries
mint leaves, to decorate

Approximately per portion:
280 kJ/67 kcal
1 g protein, 0 g fat
16 g carbohydrate
1 g fibre

Approximate preparation time: about 3$^1/_2$ hours of which 3 hours are freezing time

1. Pour boiling water over the peaches, then plunge them into cold water. Peel, quarter and stone them. Put the peaches, together with the honey, half the fruit juice and the lemon juice, in a food processor and process to make a smooth purée.

2. Put the purée into a freezer-proof bowl, cover and put it into the freezer. Leave the sorbet to set for about 3 hours, but during this period beat it vigorously with a whisk two or three times to break up the ice crystals.

3. Put the teabags in a bowl and add the boiling water. Set aside for about 10 minutes to infuse. Remove the teabags, mix the tea with the remaining fruit juice and chill in the refrigerator. Chill the berries in the refrigerator.

4. Serve the sorbet in stemmed glasses and top with the berries. Pour the fruit tea mixture over the sorbet, decorate with mint leaves and serve at once.

Difficult to choose here!
Above: Refreshing Peach sorbet
Below: Fruit salad with yogurt sauce

Oats with fruit

Easy

Serves 4
115 g/4 oz wholemeal oat flakes
750 ml/1 1/4 pints water
120 ml/4 fl oz milk
115 g/4 oz prunes
2 eating apples, about 300 g/11 oz
50 g/2 oz currants
105 ml/7 tablespoons double cream
30 ml/2 tablespoons honey
75 g/3 oz chopped nuts, such as almonds or hazelnuts
salt

Approximately per portion:
2,000 kJ/480 kcal
9 g protein, 23 g fat
61 g carbohydrate
9 g fibre

- Approximate preparation time: 30 minutes

1. Put the oat flakes, water, milk and a pinch of salt into a saucepan and bring to the boil. Cover and simmer over a very low heat for 10 minutes. Stir the mixture frequently because the oat flakes easily stick to the bottom of the saucepan.

2. Meanwhile, chop the prunes. Core and coarsely grate or dice the apples.

3. Divide the oats between individual plates and top with the apple, prunes and currants. Pour over the cream and honey and sprinkle with nuts.

Soft fruit jelly

Quick

Serves 4
800 g/1 3/4 lb mixed fresh berries
250 ml/8 fl oz unsweetened fruit juice
2.5 ml/1/2 teaspoon agar-agar
50 g/2 oz raw sugar
strip of lemon rind
150 ml/1/4 pint double cream
120 ml/4 fl oz milk

Approximately per portion:
1,200 kJ/290 kcal
4 g protein, 14 g fat
37 g carbohydrate
9 g fibre

- Approximate preparation time: 30 minutes
- Chilling time: about 6 hours

1. Divide the berries between four bowls or deep plates.

2. Mix 45 ml/3 tablespoons of the fruit juice with the agar-agar. Put the remaining fruit juice, the sugar and lemon rind in a saucepan and bring to the boil. Stir in the agar-agar mixture and boil over a low heat for about 1 minute. Pour the hot mixture over the berries. Cover and chill in the refrigerator for about 6 hours.

3. Mix together the cream and milk and serve with the fruit jelly.

Tip

Agar-agar is a useful vegetarian alternative to gelatine. It is obtained from several varieties of seaweed, including *Gelidium japonicom*. It is processed into thin, white, translucent sheets and is sold in sheets and strips. It may be used for both sweet and savoury vegetarian dishes.

Above: A substantial dessert or breakfast: Oats with fruit.
Below: A light dessert – Soft fruit jelly.

INDEX AND RECIPES

Great Little Cook Books

Vegetarian Cooking

Published originally under the title *Vegetarisch genießen* by Gräfe und Unzer Verlag GmbH, München

This edition published in 2001 by Advanced Marketing, Bicester, Oxfordshire.

Translation:
Translate-A-Book, Oxford

Editing:
Linda Doeser

Typesetting:
Organ Graphic, Abingdon

10 9 8 7 6 5 4 3
Printed in Dubai

ISBN 1 901683 42 7

All statements in this book giving information and advice are believed to be true and accurate at the time of going to press, but neither the author, the translator, or the publishers can accept legal responsibility for errors or omissions.

Important advice

If possible, buy only cleaned cereals. They should not contain dust or weed seeds. The same goes for ergot, which is appearing more frequently again nowadays. It derives from a fungus that particularly attacks rye. The violet-black ergot, snow-white on the inside, is similar to a greatly enlarged slightly bent grain of the cereal. Consumed in quantity (between 5–10 g) it causes life-threatening poisoning. However the danger is relatively small if you buy cleaned cereals, as recommended.

Never eat raw pods or seeds of pulses. They contain a natural poison, phasin, which can only be rendered harmless by thorough cooking. In beansprouts this poison is only partly broken down. So you should not eat beansprouts too often and they should always be briefly heated or blanched.

Note:
Quantities for all recipes are given in both metric and imperial measures and, if appropriate, in standard measuring spoons. They are not interchangeable, so readers should follow one set or the other.
5 ml = 1 teaspoon
15 ml = 1 tablespoon

Dr Barbara Rias-Bucher
was born in Munich. After studying she worked as an editor for a Munich publisher. Since 1979 she has been a freelance food journalist for newspapers and book publishers. She has been involved with the subject of whole foods for many years, out of conviction reinforced by positive experiences. She is the author of a number of books and has been particularly praised for the high quality of her vegetarian recipes.

Odette Teubner
was taught by her father, the internationally renowned food photographer, Christian Teubner. After that she worked for some months as a fashion photographer. At present she works exclusively in the Teubner Studio for Food Photography. In her spare time she is an enthusiastic painter of children's portraits. She uses her own son as a model.

Kerstin Mosny
studied photography at a college in French-speaking Switzerland. After that she worked as an assistant to various photographers, including the food photographer, Jürgen Tapprich in Zürich. Most recently she has been working in the Teubner Studio for Food Photography.